In Quiet,
Come Answers

learn the power of journaling

Learn the process and benefits of journaling and how it can make a difference. In quiet come answers, and that is not all……

By Miriam Ezell
Certified Christian Life Coach

Balboa Press books may be ordered through booksellers or by contacting:

Balboa Press
A Division of Hay House
1663 Liberty Drive
Bloomington, IN 47403
www.balboapress.com
844-682-1282

ISBN: 979-8-7652-3304-7 (sc)
ISBN: 979-8-7652-3305-4 (e)

Library of Congress Control Number: 2022915137

Print information available on the last page.

Balboa Press rev. date: 11/16/2022

BALBOA.PRESS
A DIVISION OF HAY HOUSE

It has been over twenty years since I started journaling and teaching workshops.

Just want to say thank you...

To the women who came to the workshops—
those who were seeking a tool to use for personal development,
healing, peace, and more. It is because of you that I
realized the need to keep talking about journaling. By
putting this guide together, the knowledge will be put into more hands
and souls that need the precious gift of quiet.

To my wonderful husband, who continues to
encourage and inspire me.

To my friends, who show up at these workshops
time and time again because they love to hang out
with other spiritual women, to learn, and to grow.

To my Creator, who placed this desire on my heart
to share the journaling process. Since the desire to share
the journaling process would not go
away, I *knew* I had to do something with it.
To God be the glory! Amen.

"It's a difficult lesson to learn today—to leave one's friends and family and deliberately practice the art of solitude [quiet] for an hour or a day or a week. And yet, once it is done, I find there is a quality to being alone that is incredibly precious. Life rushes back into the void, richer, more vivid, fuller than before."[1]

—Anne Morrow Lindbergh
(Author of "Gift from the Sea", wife of Charles
Lindbergh and mother of five children)

---

[1] Anne Morrow Lindbergh, *Gift from the Sea* (New York: Random House, 1991), 36.

How to Use This Workbook

This workbook is designed to be a personal development tool to teach you the basics of journaling: how to engage in the experience and how it can make a difference in your life.

This workbook walks you through how to create your environment for journaling, discusses the benefits of journaling, and takes you through some simple exercises.

It is designed to help you become a better you, to help you find strength, confidence, and wisdom. You are not here just to settle, you are not here on this earth just to survive—*you* are here to *thrive*.

By thriving, you will have a way to handle stress, to stop the noise in your head, to heal, to gain courage and confidence, and to find peace.

Who doesn't need or want that, right?

Still have questions?

Interested in having a workshop?

Reach out to mezell506@gmail.com

Contents

Sharing My Story

In my early forties, a combination of events forced me to take a good, hard look at myself—and I did not like what I saw.

I finally realized that the doctors were right: I was never going to get pregnant and have children. I had known that for years. But in the back of my mind, I was saying to myself, *You don't know my God. My God performs miracles. If He wants me to have children, it is going to happen.* So there, I was, looking for a miracle that did **not** happen.

Not being a mom and being part of a community and church, where family was the main focus, was very hard. I began to hate Christmas because Christmas was for kids. I refused to decorate and put up a tree. If my husband's mom were not so into Christmas, my choice would be to disappear and hide on December 1 and not come out until January 3.

Mother's Day and Father's Day were extremely hard on us as a couple. We would **not** attend church services on those days. We would do something else instead. My husband began to call Mother's Day "Mimi Day," and plan something special, just for me.

Realizing I would not be a mom, I started asking myself who I was supposed to be. *If I was not going to raise children, then what was my role in this world?*

At the same time, my husband and I had just completed working with our church youth group. We had been devoted to these kids for ten years, as "huddle" leaders. Then we stopped. We thought we were no longer *effective.* When we stopped working with teens, I lost my *ministry.* I lost my *purpose.* These church kids were filling a void.

At this time, I was working in my own CPA practice, and I was at a crossroads. Either I would hire more people to grow the practice or I would merge with another practice. I was bored and needed a stretch.

All of these things culminated in a crossroads of feeling lost, out of sorts, and directionless.

Then, I received a phone call from an elder at our church. He was actually calling me for a character reference on a gentleman he was getting ready to hire. I asked about the job the gentleman was applying for. It was the vice president of finance. After listening to the job description, I said, "I might be interested in this job!"

He said, "Great. Send me your resume."

And I did.

That phone call led to a new path. Several months later, I was closing down my practice and "stretching" myself into a new position as VP of Finance. I was in my early forties and thinking, *Wow, what an opportunity, to have this role, what an honor, and what a privilege—more responsibility and growth.*

Because this opportunity came to me, surely this was what God meant for me to do! Surely, this was my purpose.

After several years of getting settled in, going through three lawsuits, dealing with cash flow issues, losing a contract, and having to lay off employees, the gnawing in my belly saying, *This is* not *my purpose*—the *restlessness*—came back.

With all of these things going on in my life, Satan was attacking hard, putting thoughts into my head. The recorder in my head was playing, *You are not a mom because you would make a terrible mother. No blessings for you. You are not worthy.* I was falling into a pit of depression.

I knew the scripture that said God had a plan for me. I knew the right thing to do was trust God. Nevertheless, I could not pull myself out of this dark cloud.

I found myself driving to work one day, hitting the steering wheel with my fist, crying, and saying out loud to the Lord, "This is not what you promised. This is not what you promised."

When I stopped having my little tantrum, I heard the scripture in my head: "For I know the plans I have for you, [*Miriam*], plans to make you prosper and not for evil, plans to give you a future and a hope. That when you call upon me and pray to me, I will hear you. And when you seek me, you will find me."

I said out loud, "Lord, I know that verse, but I have no clue what plans you have for me. I am in my forties, halfway through my life. And I still have no idea what plans you have for me. I am clueless. I am directionless."

When things settled down again, in the quiet, these words came back at me: "Well go out and find it!"

I yelled back, "OK, I will!" (end of story)

Well, how do you do that—*go out and "find" it?*

How do you find your calling—the "plans" that are just for you?

How does that happen?

What does that mean?

What does that look like?

All of these questions were swarming in my head.

Interestingly, my mother was going through the process of reinventing herself at the age of sixty. After divorcing my dad and creating a new life, she had to figure out who she was as this single woman.

Soon after my incident in the car, I went home for a visit to spend time with mom. She was so excited about a book she was reading, and was creating a "vision board". She was giving herself permission for personal development and working on just her. *What? Tell me more.*

She was reading *Simple Abundance: 365 Days to a Balanced and Joyful Life* by Sarah Ban Breathnach. It was written for women over forty, to help them find their authentic selves. Then I remembered that I received that book as a birthday gift, years ago, from a precious friend. I had that book but never really paid much attention to it.

Let me back up here for just a minute. When I was growing up, it was all about serving—serving the church, serving family, and serving others— serve, serve, serve. It was not about me. My grandmother's motto was "you do what you have to do." For my grandmother, it was not about you and self-development or focusing on your purpose, strengths, desires, and passion. It was about duty and serving the church.

Don't get me wrong. There is a time and a place for serving others. Do I want you to serve? Absolutely. But in the capacity of love, desire, connection and not in the capacity of "duty" and showing up with an unpleasant attitude. Knowing who you are and what you do best plays a role in your desire to serve.

That weekend, mom introduced me to a new concept that I did not even know existed. Finding your authentic self, self-care—what were those? You can spend time on yourself, really? This was so foreign to me.

I thought about this on my flight home. Wow, if mom was doing this, maybe I should give it a try. I was searching and I had not found a way to get answers—*yet*. I really did not know who I was and what I should be doing with my life. I felt like there was so much more out there.

Then I thought, *What would my husband think if I started working on myself? Would he think it was selfish?*

I knew I had to do something. If this book, *Simple Abundance*, could help me, then I was going to try.

Reading this book started a morning routine of getting up early, reading my Bible and then reading the daily thought out of *Simple Abundance*. This book, *Simple Abundance*, was so impactful that I could not wait to get up the next morning and read the next day's thought.

Each page in the book had a thought. Each thought was teaching me how to ask myself questions, for example: *What do I want? What do I need to live a simple life?*

This book was teaching me about gratitude, simplicity, order, harmony, beauty, and joy. It was teaching me how to include these attributes in my daily life—to be authentic to me.

Authentic to me means finding my voice, my core values, what makes it important to me.

As a result of these basic probing questions, I was on a search to find my calling/purpose. I started asking myself questions, such as: *What do I enjoy doing? What am I doing or working on when time flies by? What is my passion?*

I would write questions in a journal and answer them honestly. The questions kept coming, and I would ask and write, ask and write. Going deeper in the process. Peeling away the layers of the onion. That was the process of journaling: just writing down the question, on the page, and answering it honestly, on the page.

What did I learn over the years about journaling?

I gave myself permission to work on me. I gave myself the "gift" of time: to take time out, work on me, and figure this out. I also learned how to:

> think and process;
> feel;
> find answers;
> seek my true self;
> find my voice; and
> lay it all on the page, raw and honest.

In the following pages of this guide, I will teach you the benefits of journaling, show you how to set up the environment for journaling, and walk you through some exercises so you can experience the journaling process.

It is my hope that the journaling process leads *you* to a life of purpose and meaning, direction and clarity, and that it really makes a difference in your life.

Blessings, my friend,

Miriam

Getting Comfortable with Quiet

Being quiet is hard. Being still is hard. As women, we are on the move constantly, and there is a lot of noise going on in our heads. The noise can range from what to cook for supper to the negative voice that says, "You are not good enough."

Journaling/being quiet is your time. Recognize this as a gift to yourself. I recommend starting out by spending five to fifteen minutes being quiet, feeling it, and experiencing it. I know this is uncomfortable and not easy, but you can do this. Here are some suggestions to help.

1. Go outside for a solo walk, without ear buds. Listen to nature and observe the beautiful variations of colors and textures. What do you smell? What do you see? What do you hear?

2. Sit outside with nature and write in your journal, taking notes of what you see, smell, and hear. Be descriptive. Not just *I hear a bird singing*, but rather something like, *I hear a bird singing a sweet melody.* Describe colors and textures.

3. Sit some place quiet and grab your beautiful journal. With a blank page staring at you, start writing what is in your head. I call this "data dumping." Write everything that comes to mind from groceries that need to be picked up to the negative thoughts about you and who you are.

4. Stop talking out loud and write on paper. Resist the urge to have a conversation with someone. Just get away.

5. Be in the moment. Put the cell phone away, turn off the TV, stop the distractions. Sit and listen for five minutes.

6. Breathe. Breathe in and out. Concentrate. Breathe deeply. It is when we breathe in and out that we can clear our minds.

7. Start with gratitude. Grab that beautiful journal and spend a few quiet moments writing the things for which you are grateful, such as a car that starts in the morning so you can get where you need to be.

8. Doodle. With pen and journal, make circles, squares, lines, stick figure people, or write your favorite words. Just feel the pen move in your hand without any purpose; practice doodling in quiet.

9. Read a book. Get lost in a book with your imagination and let the world live without you.

You need silence to recharge your battery. Get away from those moments where you are being asked a million questions.

Now reflect. What did you learn about yourself through the experience of quiet? How did that work for you? Was it easy or hard to stay quiet?

Tom Carrol posted on YouTube a video called "30 days of journaling made my life better." Here is what he says.

Journal writing is also a form of meditation. It forces you to slow down and focus on one thing for an extended period of time. Different types of meditation can potentially decrease stress and have positive effects on your ability to control attention, to regulate your emotions, and to have self-awareness. It causes actual changes to the make-up of your brain. Journaling can also help with your physical health, can actually strengthen your immune system and speed up healing times from injuries.

Understanding the Benefits of Journaling

Self-Reflection

Make time for self-reflection and awareness. Stop the treadmill and breathe; spend time reflecting. Why self-reflection? You learn more about yourself: how you handle situations, how your emotions show up, what you do well, what you would like to do better.

Jot down notes of what happened during the day or the previous day and what would you do differently. This leads to discovering more about you and your makeup.

Self-reflection is a time for you to be honest with yourself; one of my clients even called it "raw." Knowing more of who you are and why you do the things you do also helps with your confidence.

Gain Clarity

Put on paper whatever is on your mind for that day. Write. Write. Write. Getting it out of your head and onto the page helps clear your mind, organize your thoughts, and so on. In the book *The Artist's Way,* Julia Cameron recommends writing three pages a day.[2] She refers to these pages as "morning pages." This may be a challenge to write three pages a day, but the point is, to get the stuff out of your head and onto the page.

---

[2] Julia Cameron, *The Artist's Way* (New York: Tarcher/Penguin Putnam, 1992, 2002), 10.

When you write something down, you begin to think about it, and gain clarity; being on the page makes it real. Giving the issue some time and thought helps to bring your issue into focus.

Matt D'Avella shared this on his YouTube video "What I learned by journaling for 30 days."

The one small benefit I saw, early on, was that it helped with my perfectionism. As a chronic overthinker, it was therapeutic in a way to just write what was on my mind without the chance to edit later. It helped me to accept how I was feeling. It stopped me from running away from the thoughts I was having or pretending they didn't exist. Among many other things, journaling has been a helpful tool for me to gain clarity when my mental health was at its worst.

Gain Strength

In quietness and in confidence is your strength.
—Isaiah 30:15 (NLT)

When I was a VP of Finance, we had three lawsuits going on at the same time. If any one of these three was awarded to the plantiff, we were done. We would be put out of business. You can imagine the stress since I was in charge of cash flow and payroll.

As I journaled, I found myself day after day giving these lawsuits to the Lord. By that, I mean I defined my situation, put my stress on the page, and talked to the Lord about them. I would write, "I am giving this to you, Lord. I am asking for your guidance and strength and that these lawsuits are resolved by this date." I would actually tell the Lord a date that they be resolved.

By doing this, I could feel myself sit up taller, giving me the capacity and the strength to carry the load. I would arrive at work refreshed and ready to face the day. "Bring it on" is what I would say aloud as I drove to work. I knew God was with me and this situation; knowing that He was in charge—not *me*—gave me so much peace.

Solve Problems

Write down the problem or situation you are dealing with, claim it, and name it. Then address the problem, asking yourself, *What is the right next step for me?* Write down what comes to mind. Answer that question on your page. What thoughts, ideas, or comments come to mind? Have you ever dealt with something like this before? How did you handle it?

To be honest, I had a coaching client and this was her assignment: to write down the answer to that question: "What is the right next step for me?" She did not get an answer while sitting and journaling. However, the next day on her way to work the answer came as she was *quietly* driving. She parked her car, rushed into her office, grabbed her Day-Timer (because that was the only paper she had at the moment) and wrote three pages.

I have had incidents where the answer comes while I am taking a shower or standing at the sink washing dishes.

If an answer does not come as fast as you would like, be patient. Think of your problem as a growth area and ask, "What am I to learn from this experience?" Keep journaling. Keep asking the same question until you have clarity or peace around it. Do not be discouraged.

Reach a Goal

There is something about putting a goal on paper that makes it come to fruition. I cannot define the "secret sauce" or explain how it happens. I just know it happens.

After you write it down, you will begin to hear things that relate to your goal. Someone will mention a book that you need to read, YouTube videos that you need to watch will show up in your YouTube search. Could it be that your awareness is heightened and, since it is out of your head and on the page, it is in the forefront?

Better Communication

Since you are writing in your own words and formulating sentences, journaling will help with communication skills, such as email writing.

With pen to paper, write out and prepare for conversations around a particular situation. This also makes you a better communicator, especially when it is time to have a crucial conversation at work or home.

When I talk with my clients about a difficult conversation they need to have, I encourage them to write out the scenario on paper: what would they say, how would the individual respond, what would they say to that. Play out the conversation while writing it on paper. Writing it out and thinking it through prepares you for the conversation giving you more peace and confidence.

Feel Peace

Write it down, and give it to Jesus. Let it go! I know that is hard; you want to be in control of the situation. May I remind you that it is not for you to carry this burden.

As a result of giving it to Jesus, burdens will be lifted off your shoulders. You will feel lighter, you will stand up taller—just like I experienced in my example earlier.

Words from Jesus found in John 14:27 (NLT): "I am leaving you with a gift–peace of mind and heart. And the peace I give is a gift the world cannot give. So don't be troubled or afraid."

Find Connection

This is where you connect with your Heavenly Father, your Creator, your Jesus, your Lord (I use all these names synonymously). Scripture says, "When you seek my face, you will find me."

How do I seek him (Jesus)? To me, journaling is the answer. By spending time with him, you share your dreams, goals, struggles, and so on. You spend time with him. You develop that relationship. Please know that Jesus wants to be included in every area of your life. Every aspect of your life. Include him.

Julia Cameron, in her book, *The Artist's Way*, says it beautifully: "morning [journaling] pages symbolize our willingness to speak to and hear from God. They lead us into many other changes that also come from God and lead us to God. This is the hand of God moving through your hand as you write. It is very powerful."[3]

---

[3] Cameron, *Artist's Way*, 85.

Defining the Environment

You think, *Duh. How difficult could this be to figure out? Find a chair, take a pen, and a journal, and just start writing.*

I know. I just wanted to share what has worked for me to give you some insight and to highlight what I think is important for this journaling practice.

1. Choose a *quiet place.* **This is where you go to meet your Creator and spend time. I have a recliner that is comfortable in the living room, and there is good lighting. If it is cold, I take one of my quilts to keep me warm. It is early morning before anyone else is up and about. I choose mornings since I am a morning person and can think more clearly.**

   As I began this process, and after journaling for several months sitting in this same place, I could head in that direction and an overwhelming sense of peace consumed me. I declared it "my sacred space."

   I make sure all is quiet. The dishwasher is not running; the washing machine is not on. I do not have my cell phone or iPad with me. You get the picture: avoid distractions.

   Maybe in nice weather you want to create a sacred space outside on your porch and listen to the sounds of nature. That definitely works too.

   Find out what works for you. Get away from the distractions and the noise.

   What does your "sacred space" look like? How can you create this?

2. Choose your favorite writing utensil. **Again, *Duh*. I am serious. I have colored pens that I picked up from a craft store. I write with a thin**

pen because it is the most comfortable in my hand. I write with a thin tip because the letters and words look pretty on the page.

If I write down a scripture, I will use a gold pen that reflects and glimmers on the page and reminds me of His glory.

So, what pen do you like to hold in your hand that feels best as you put pen to paper?

3. Choose a journal. To me, this is the fun part. Each year I start with a new journal. Mine needs to be lined because I cannot write in straight lines on a blank page, and the lines are wide enough for me to write big.

I have one friend whose choice is more of an art journal with blank pages. She actually journals with images and doodles pictures and words. I am not that creative.

My journal cover has to be pretty. The journal speaks to me and wants to be held and opened.

I will buy my journals from a gift shop, from a bookstore, from online sources, or even make my own from an inexpensive English composition book and decorate the cover. I will share more about that under the creative part of this guide.

Go explore and find a journal that resonates with you.

4. Choose your favorite beverage. tea, coffee, Diet Coke, or something else. This makes the environment and experience relaxing. It helps set the tone.

5. Choose your time of day. Are you a morning person with less distractions in the morning? Do you prefer journaling at the end of your work day before you leave the office? How about before you go to bed at night? The choice is yours.

It is an investment in you. Take five to thirty minutes to be still and journal. I know you are busy. I am not putting this on your plate to stress you out, to tell you that you *have* to do this or *else*. This is simply a tool to be used to help you. I do not journal every day, but when I do, it takes about fifteen to thirty minutes. When I do journal, it is in the morning and I find my day goes better; I have more peace and patience to deal with things that show up. I feel ready to face the day. I am more organized.

This is for you to experience. I think once you start and see the benefits, it will be hard **not** to journal. Journal as needed.

After I presented a workshop, an individual asked me if she could type and journal on her computer. My suggestion is that taking pen to paper is more effective. Putting pen to paper makes it more raw and more real. Having a beautiful journal with your own handwriting, even the misspelled words or cross outs, make it more authentic to you.

These are the basics to defining your journaling environment. Now take these suggestions and customize what works for you.

Journaling is where you are most honest with yourself.
Be RAW.

Practicing the Journaling Process

Here we go. Let's get the wheels turning. Grab your journal and let's practice the journaling process of questions and answers.

Just write. Take your time. I encourage you to write as much as you can to answer the questions below. Let the words be descriptive and spill onto the page. Spend time on your answers. Enjoy the process.

For the beginner:

- Where is my favorite vacation spot, and what makes it my favorite?
- What does fun look like to me? What do I do for fun? When was the last time I had fun?
- Who am I?
- What is my skill set or abilities?
- What did I do as a child at the age of ten or twelve that kept me busy?
- What would hold me back from journaling?
- What could I do to remove those obstacles and to experience the power of journaling?

For the advanced:

- What am I doing when I get lost in the moment and time flies?
- What do I want? What do I need?
- If a magic wand was waved over my head tonight, and tomorrow I woke up and things were different, what would that look like?
- If money and time were not a factor, what would I do?
- If I were given a microphone and a podium to speak to the world, what would be my message? What makes that important to me?
- What do I want my legacy to be?
- If I could do it over again, what would I do differently?
- How would my world be different if I was walking in alignment with God's plan for me?
- My "perfect" day would be...

- What experience has affected my life the most?
- What am I doing when I feel most alive?

For healing:
- What can I do for rest?
- Who can I talk to who would listen and help me process these emotions?
- What do I need to write today to just get my emotions on the page?
- What am I learning about myself during this time of healing?
- Write down affirmations—change the negative thoughts into positive ones. Positive statements such as; I am confident. I am creative. I can do this.
- Imagine being on vacation. Describe what you see, hear, feel. Embrace the imagination and relax.

For confidence:
- Who in my life do I need to spend more time with who has a positive attitude?
- Who in my life do I **not** need to spend time with because that person is dragging me down?
- What can I do that is out of my comfort zone, that will stretch me and give me confidence? If I can do X, I can do anything, right?
- Who exudes confidence that I admire? What are the person's attributes? How can I spend time with that person and get to know him or her better?

For peace:
- Where can I go that exudes a peaceful environment?
- How and when can I give myself permission to take time out to practice peace, quiet, and journaling?
- How can I make my environment more peaceful at home? At work?
- What in my home or work space is bringing stress into my life? What can I do to change that?

Taking a Deeper Dive Experience

Let's go deeper. Putting pen to paper, write down this question:

> Heavenly Father, Creator of all things, what do you need to teach me today?

With pen to paper, wait patiently. Then start writing what comes out of your heart onto the page. What is the answer?

Remember Julia Cameron's words from *The Artist's Way*: "morning [journaling] pages symbolize our willingness to speak to and hear from God. They lead us into many other changes that also come from God and lead us to God. This is the hand of God moving through your hand as you write. It is very powerful."[4]

---

[4] Cameron, *Artist's Way,* 85.

Learning to Play Again— Creativity as a Form of Quiet

During my self-discovery journey, I found that I desired to be creative. It started when I visited with my mother and she was taking watercolor lessons. I was fascinated by that and asked for a demonstration. While she demonstrated, pink roses came alive right in front of me. I was hooked. For Christmas that year, she gave me watercolor brushes and paints. Then I found a local teacher and started taking lessons. I found myself getting lost in the moment, which is another way to be still and quiet, and recharge my battery.

Why creativity? Because it gives you the opportunity to step out of the ordinary. Get away from your role: the role of mother, employee, boss, neighbor, daughter, or wife. You need something to help you forget about yourself for a while—to momentarily forget your problems, your age, your duties, your failures, and all that you have lost or screwed up. You need something that takes you away so that you can get lost in the moment, where time flies by. Do something you love, take time to explore, to get lost, to try something without expectations, and just be in the moment. Being creative is *a time to become a kid again.*

While creating and getting lost in the moment, you are creating a moment of peace and love toward something. This is also a time to connect with your Heavenly Father, artist to artist.

This is where the fun begins and you can get creative with your journal. When I started teaching the journaling workshops, I wanted other women to experience "being creative" and "getting lost in the moment." I supplied English composition journals that I found at an office supply store, took magazines, scrapbooking paper, ribbons, buttons, scissors, and glue and gave them the opportunity and time to decorate their own journals.

It took them about an hour to customize and complete their journals.

Here is an example of an English composition journal with a decorated cover that I created. The little girl on the front is a picture of my mom at four years old. I like the theme "Unlimited Possibilities"—that really resonated with me.

In this example, the women used scrapbooking paper to customize their journals.

Speaking of being creative, here is another idea when it comes to your creativity. Maybe during your journaling time a theme shows up: travel, cooking, nature, or home décor.

Now it is time to think about a vision board. Do you find yourself dreaming about something in the future? Create a *vision board* around what you want.

Buy a piece of poster board and create a vision board. When I was on my self-discovery journey, I found I was drawn to the beach and I wanted a beach house. You will find that after you create your vision board and put it up where you can see it, often your vision becomes a reality.

Here is my vision board from years ago. It was created around the desire to own a beach house. This vision became a reality two years after the vision board was hung in my office where I could see it almost every day.

Sharing My Life-Changing Experience

At the age of fifty, I left corporate America to start my own coaching business. Of course, it started out flat. As a result, I told my husband how I was going to spend the day: I would unplug from the computer and cell phone, sit with my Bible and business magazines, and journal all day. I was looking for clarity and the next step.

At 8:00 a.m., I went to the side porch and sat outside in a comfortable chair. It was a beautiful day in the month of September and the weather was just perfect. I was looking for inspiration and answers for growing my business.

By 2:00 p.m., I still had no idea on what to do next to get my business rolling. At that time, in my journal, I asked the Lord, *What is my next step?* Right away, with pen to paper, came the response that I was to call Beltline Church of Christ in Decatur, Alabama and ask to speak at their next women's retreat. These were very specific instructions.

Why Beltline? Because I had been speaking in Cuba on a mission trip with a group of women from this church, I knew them. I reached out to my contact at Beltline and she told me who to get in touch with regarding the women's retreat. I contacted the woman at Beltline Church of Christ over Women Ministries and she told me, "Interesting that you are calling because we are meeting on Sunday to talk about our spring women's retreat."

Did you get that? My call was spot on and very timely. Was God working behind the scenes? I think so.

That next spring, I spoke at their retreat and told my story of leaving corporate America to start my coaching business. I also introduced the power of journaling. After I spoke, a woman approached me and said I needed to call her boss who owned a coaching business. Whoa!

Whenever someone tells me I need to call someone or get in touch with someone, I take that seriously. That is a direct download from my Creator.

The following Monday, I did just that and reached out to her boss who is a co-owner in a coaching business. I interviewed and was hired to be a coach and a facilitator with their organization. I have been with that company now for over six years. It was just what I needed. I needed to feel part of a team. I needed a place where I could learn and grow, and that is exactly what has been happening.

I am convinced I would not be with this team and would not have had the opportunity if I did not journal to solve my problem or get clarity or direction regarding my business.

This was *my* experience. Your Creator wants to do the *same for you and with you*. As I said before, he wants to be a part of every aspect of your life.

Amen.

As I close out this guide, I sit in my quiet time and think how can I best summarize this guide and what do I want you, as the reader, to walk away with, I journal. I ask the Lord the same question – what do you want these women to walk away with from reading this guide?

Here are the words that flowed through my hand, *pen to paper*:

> I want these women to know that I love them, they are cherished. No need is too great or too small to come to me and ask. Spend time with me.

Wow! What an answer – spend time with your Creator. Ask. No need is too great or too small. With pen to paper, what is **your** request? Your Creator is waiting to be still and quiet with you.

Remember: *In quiet, come answers.*

Searching for More - Recommended Reading

Gift from the Sea by Anne Morrow Lindbergh
The description from Amazon.com is as follows.

> Drawing inspiration from the shells on the shore, Lindbergh's musings on the shape of a woman's life will bring new understanding to readers, male and female, at any stage of life. A mother of five and professional writer, she casts an unsentimental eye at the trappings of modern life that threaten to overwhelm us—the timesaving gadgets that complicate our lives, the overcommitments that take us from our families—and by recording her own thoughts in a brief escape from her everyday demands, she guides her readers to find a space for contemplation and creativity in their own lives.

Since I am a beach lover, her words particularly spoke to me.

Simple Abundance: 365 Days to a Balanced and Joyful Life by Sarah Ban Breathnach
The description from Amazon.com is as follows.

> First published in 1995, Simple Abundance topped the New York Times Bestseller list for over two years and is responsible for introducing two hugely popular concepts— the "Gratitude Journal" and the term "Authentic Self." With daily inspirational meditations and reflections, the Simple Abundance phenomenon became a touchstone for a generation of women, helping them to reclaim their true selves, find balance during life's busiest moments, and rediscover what makes them truly happy.

This is the book I used on my self-discovery journey to find my authenticity. I could not wait to get up in the morning and read this book, to discover, to explore, and to give myself permission to work on me. It literally changed my life; it made me a better wife, daughter, and friend.

365 Journaling Writing Ideas by Rossi Fox
If you feel intimated by a blank journal page, this is the book to get your pump primed.

Bibliography

Cameron, Julia. *The Artist's Way.* New York: Tarcher/Penguin Putnam, 1992, 2002.

Lindbergh, Anne Morrow. *Gift from the Sea.* New York: Random House, 1991.

Printed in the United States
by Baker & Taylor Publisher Services